Counting with an Abacus

Learning the Place Values of Ones, Tens, and Hundreds

Patricia J. Murphy

Math
for the
REAL World™

Rosen Classroom Books & Materials
New York

Published in 2004 by The Rosen Publishing Group, Inc.
29 East 21st Street, New York, NY 10010

Copyright © 2004 by The Rosen Publishing Group, Inc.

Book Design: Ron A. Churley

Photo Credits: Cover © Ken Reid/Taxi; p. 5 © Bettmann/Corbis; pp. 6, 13 (photo) © Keren Su/Corbis;
pp. 7, 9, 10, 11, 13 (abacuses) by Ron A. Churley; p. 12 © James Marshall/Corbis.

ISBN: 0-8239-8880-5
6-pack ISBN: 0-8239-7389-1

Manufactured in the United States of America

Contents

What Is an Abacus?

An abacus is a tool used to count and do math problems. An abacus has 3 main parts: a top **deck**, a bottom deck, and a **crossbar**. An abacus also has a **frame**, long rods, and colored beads. As the beads on an abacus are counted, they are moved to the crossbar. Beads in the bottom deck are moved up to reach the crossbar. Beads in the top deck are moved down to reach the crossbar.

Chinese people made the first abacus around 500 B.C.! The picture on page 5 shows a modern abacus.

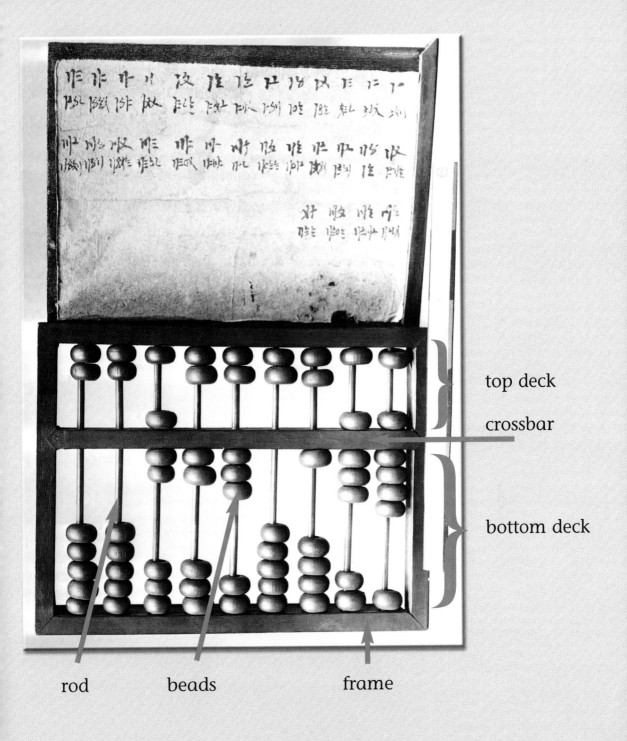

top deck

crossbar

bottom deck

rod   beads   frame

The Place-Value System

Our numbers are based on the **place-value system**. The value of each **digit** depends on where it is in the number. The rods of an abacus stand for the places in our place-value system. The first rod on the right side of an abacus stands for the ones place. The next rod stands for the tens place. The next rod stands for the hundreds place, and so on.

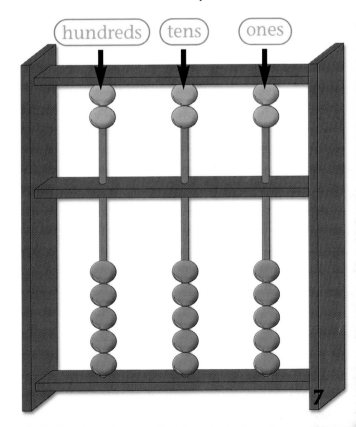

Instead of numbers, an abacus uses beads to show what digit is in each place.

The Bottom Deck

Each rod in the bottom deck of an abacus has 5 beads. The value of each bead depends on which rod it is on. Each bead on the ones rod in the bottom deck **equals** 1. Each bead on the tens rod in the bottom deck equals 10. Each bead on the hundreds rod in the bottom deck equals 100.

To count 1, move 1 bead on the ones rod up to the crossbar. To count 10, move 1 bead on the tens rod up to the crossbar. To count 100, move 1 bead on the hundreds rod up to the crossbar.

The abacus on page 9 shows the number 321. In this number, 1 is in the ones place, 2 is in the tens place, and 3 is in the hundreds place. There is 1 bead counted on the ones rod, 2 beads counted on the tens rod, and 3 beads counted on the hundreds rod.

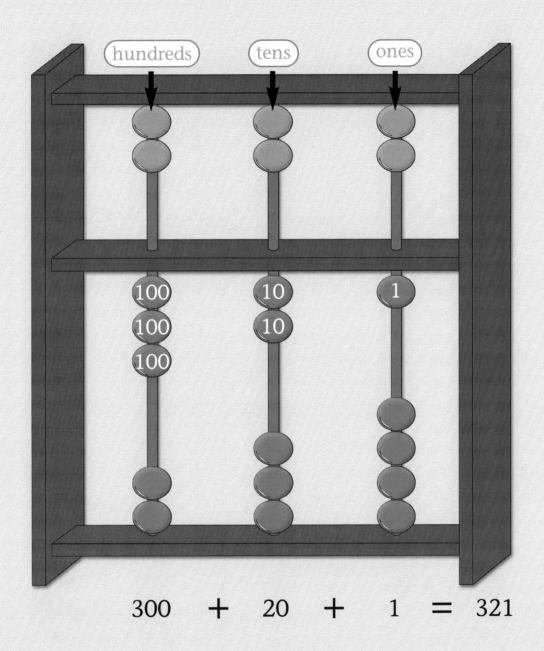

300 $+$ 20 $+$ 1 $=$ 321

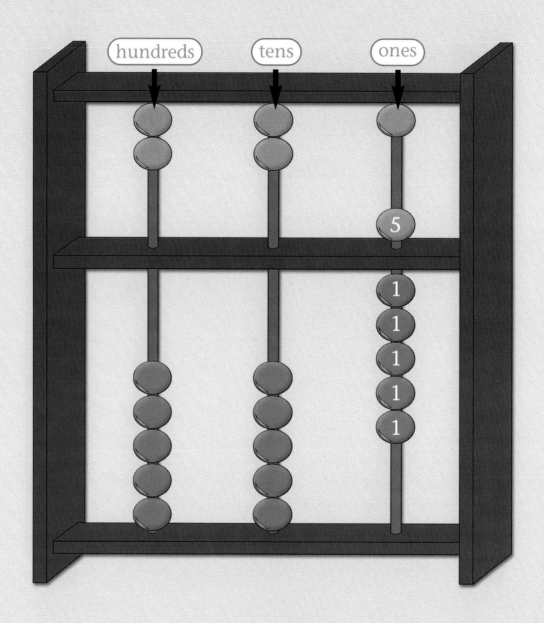

The Top Deck

Each rod in the top deck of an abacus has 2 beads. Each bead on the ones rod in the top deck equals 5. Once you have counted 5 beads on the ones rod in the bottom deck, those 5 beads can be traded for 1 bead on the ones rod in the top deck. That is because they both have the same value: 5.

Each bead on the tens rod in the top deck equals 50. Each bead on the hundreds rod in the top deck equals 500.

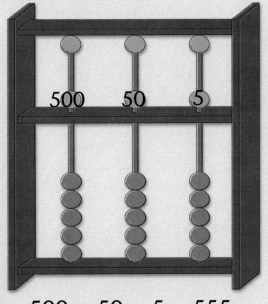

$$500 + 50 + 5 = 555$$

Each bead in the top deck is worth 5 times as much as each bead on the same rod in the lower deck. This abacus shows the number 555.

11

The Abacus Today

Today, many children in **Asia** use an abacus to learn about numbers in school. They are taught to picture an abacus in their minds. This helps them to do all kinds of math!

Some shopkeepers in Asia also use an abacus. With practice, shopkeepers and schoolchildren can work out math problems very quickly.

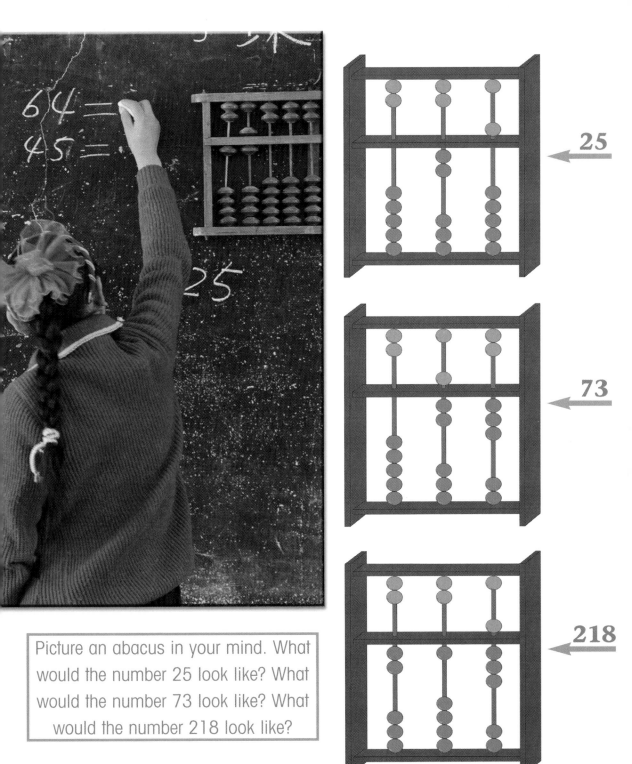

25

73

218

Picture an abacus in your mind. What would the number 25 look like? What would the number 73 look like? What would the number 218 look like?

Fun with an Abacus

You and your friends can use an abacus to play the math games listed below, or you can make up your own abacus games!

- Rock and Roll Abacus—Roll 2 dice and show the number on your abacus. Roll again and add the new number to the number already on your abacus. Keep rolling and adding until you reach 100!

- Abacus Race—Play this game with 2 friends and 2 abacuses. One friend calls out a number, and the other 2 race to see who can show it on their abacus first!

Glossary

Asia (AY-zhuh) One of Earth's 7 large landmasses.

crossbar (KROSS-bahr) The part of an abacus that divides the top deck and the bottom deck.

deck (DEHK) One of the 2 sections of an abacus where beads are moved and counted.

digit (DIH-juht) Any of the figures 0, 1, 2, 3, 4, 5, 6, 7, 8, and 9.

equals (EE-kwuhlz) To be the same as.

frame (FRAYM) The outside part of an abacus that holds the other parts together.

place-value system (PLAYSS–VAL-you SIS-tuhm) A number system in which the value of a digit depends on its place in a number. At the farthest right is the ones place. Next is the tens place, then the hundreds place, and so on.

Index